Contents

Inside illustrations by:

Peter Bailey

Ellis Nadler

Chris Mould

The Laughter Forecast

Today will be humorous
With some giggly patches.
Scattered outbreaks of chuckling in the south
And smiles spreading from the east later.
Widespread chortling
Increasing to gale force guffaws towards evening.
The outlook for tomorrow
Is hysterical.

Sue Cowling

Hippobotamus

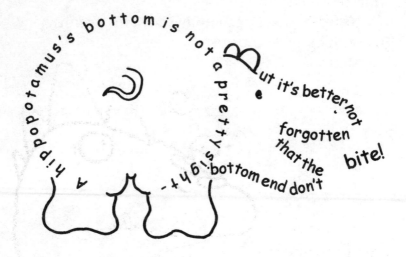

A hippopotamus's bottom is not a pretty sight - bottom end don't But it's better not forgotten that the bite!

Liz Brownlee

Well Spotted

'I've spots all over me,' she said.
'I'm positively peppered.'
'Don't worry, dear,' her mum replied.
'It's normal in a . . .

   leopard.'

Marian Swinger

The Dinosaur

I dreamt I met a dinosaur.
I stared at it and blinked.
But, looking once again, I saw
the poor thing was extinct!

Colin Macfarlane

My Newt

I have a newt called Tiny
He's really kind of cute
The reason he's called Tiny?
Quite simple. He's my newt.

Richard Caley

Brian and the Lion

Brian saw a lian
The lian was crian
Why's the lion crion?
thought Brion, sion.
Why you crion, lion? asked Brion.
I'm not crion said the lion.
You're lyan said Bryan
You're a lyan lyan!

The lion ate Brion.

Trevor Millum

A Froggy Was Sitting Crying

A froggy was sitting crying
On the kitchen floor
Looking up with tearful eyes
At the closed fridge door.

And what did froggy long for?
What was locked inside?
An ice-cold Croak-a-Cola,
That's why froggy cried . . .

Clive Webster

Just a Tad

'Come on, son,' says Dadpole,
'Don't make your dad get madpole,
You silly little ladpole,
You fussy, faddy fadpole!
Sit on the lily padpole
And eat your dinner, badpole!
Your poor old mum's a sadpole.
Make everyone a gladpole
And try to eat a tad pole.'

Maureen Haselhurst

Good Morning, Mr Croco-Doco-Dile

Good morning, Mr Croco-doco-dile,
And how are you today?
I like to see you croco-smoco-smile
In your croco-woco-way.

From the tip of your beautiful croco-toco-tail
To your croco-hoco-head
You seem to me so croco-stoco-still
As if you're croco-doco-dead.

Perhaps if I touch your croco-cloco-claw
Or your croco-snoco-snout,
Or get up close to your croco-joco-jaw
I shall very soon find out.

But suddenly I croco-soco-see
In your croco-oco-eye
A curious kind of croco-gloco-gleam,
So I just don't think I'll try.

Forgive me, Mr Croco-doco-dile
But it's time I was away.
Let's talk a little croco-woco-while
Another croco-doco-day.

Charles Causley

Octocure

Oliver the Octopus
Was feeling rather ill.
He went to see the doctopus
Who sent him for a pill.
He said, 'That's chickenpoctopus,
Your tentacles are spotty.'
Poor Olly got a shocktopus—
He felt a little dotty.
He bought four pairs of socktopus
To hide his spotty legs,
And fed himself on choctopus
And jellyfishes' eggs.
In just a week the octopus
Felt better than before.
The spots had gone—the doctopus
Had found the perfect cure.

Alison Chisholm

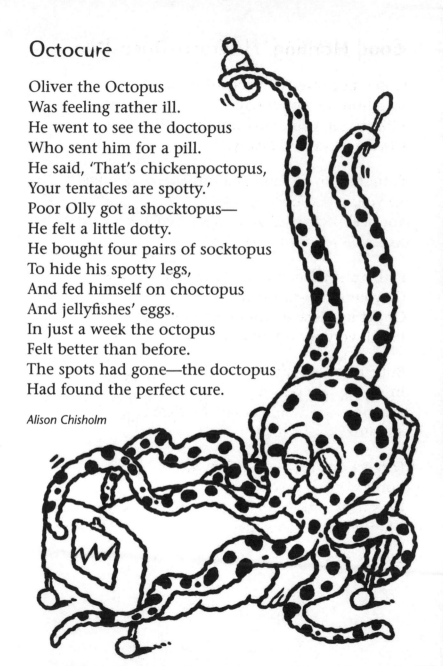

Lolly Licking

Lick a lolly
sticky lolly
lick a
l
o
l
l
i
p
o
p

Lick a lolly
tricky lolly
from the
l
o
l
l
i
s
h
o
p

Lick a lolly
sticky lolly
till it makes
y
o
u
s
i
c
k

Lick a lolly
quicky lolly
till there's
just
a

s
t
i
c
k

Ray Mather

Little Miss Muffet

Little Miss Muffet sat on a tuffet,
Eating her curds and whey.
Along came a spider who sat down beside her
And said, 'Whatcha got in the bowl, sweetheart?'

Anon.

Multi-culture

I really luv chapatties
I eat dem all de time,
Today Iqbal made ten of dem
An nine of dem were mine,
I am krazy over mangoes
I once grew a mango tree,
My mango tree grew chapatties
Especially for me.

Benjamin Zephaniah

Mother Alligator's Advice to Her Children

Don't eat too much sweet
You'll spoil your lovely teeth.

Don't touch jelly or treacle
Stick to eating people.

John Agard

Ruptured Recipe

Take a dozen little boys
Put them through a sieve,
Stew them till they thicken
Ask them where they live,
Dot them with some butter
Label them with ink,
Spread the lot with mustard
To make a pleasant drink.

Barbara Giles

Be Nice to Rhubarb

Please say a word for rhubarb,
   It hasn't many chums
For people like banana splits
   Or fancy juicy plums.

They slice the sweet, sweet melon
   Or gather tasty pears,
But if you mention rhubarb pie
   You get the *rhu*dest stares.

They praise the yellow lemon,
   The golden orange cool,
But rhubarb's never mentioned
   —Or that's the general *rhu*le.

For rhubarb stewed and blushing
   I've only this to say,
If they should cast an unkind barb
   I'll see they *rhu* the day.

Max Fatchen

Why Does Rhubarb Crumble?

I know why . . .
Cheese slices
Potato chips
Pear drops
Tomato dips
Onion rings
Sausage rolls
Banana splits
And salad bowls
But why does rhubarb crumble?

Richard Caley

Riddle

Squishy and squashy
Sometimes like toffee.
Stretched long and tall
Or rolled up in a ball.
Pummelled and pounded
Until it is rounded
Blown up full of air
It makes them all stare
Then it goes pop
And you have to stop.
There is a real mess.
Can you make a guess?
   What it is?

Margaret Blount

Answer:
Bubble Gum

Yum!

I like pepper on my ice cream;
    Some like ice cream chilly.
I put ice cubes in the tea pot;
    Boiling tea is silly.

If you want your bread to harden,
    (Hard enough to chew)
Mix the flour with best cement
    And butter it with glue.

Some folks think this poem's stupid;
    Others think they're wrong.
Set it to a little tune
    And sing it as a song.

Gerard Benson

Elephantasy

'There's been an elephant in my fridge,'
  I heard an old man mutter.
'How can you tell?' I asked him—
  'Footprints in the butter!'

'The elephant's still in there.'
  The old man gave a 'Tut!'
'How do you know?' I asked him—
  'Look, the door won't shut!'

Celia Warren

The Yeti

A yeti ate a lemon.
A yeti ate a plum.
A yeti bet a penny
that then he'd eat my mum.

I didn't mind the lemon.
I didn't mind the plum.
But I did get annoyed
when the yeti ate my mum!

Celia Warren

My Painting

Yesterday
I did a house.

Today
I think I'll do a mouse.

I think I'll paint it
Green and red,

Red for the body,
Green for the head,

And make its whiskers
Black as night

To give Miss Wilkinson
A fright!

Matt Simpson

I Don't Know What to Write

I don't
know what
to write.
My
classmates
seem much
slicker.
If I
write like
this,
I'll fill
my page
much
quicker!

Tracey Blance

Where Do All the Teachers Go?

Where do all the teachers go
When it's four o'clock?
Do they live in houses
And do they wash their socks?

Do they wear pyjamas
And do they watch TV?
And do they pick their noses
The same as you and me?

Do they live with other people?
Have they mums and dads?
And were they ever children?
And were they ever bad?

Did they ever, never spell right?
Did they ever makes mistakes?
Were they punished in the corner
If they pinched the chocolate flakes?

Did they ever lose their hymn books?
Did they ever leave their greens?
Did they scribble on the desk tops?
Did they wear old dirty jeans?

I'll follow one back home today
I'll find out what they do
Then I'll put it in a poem
That they can read to you.

Peter Dixon

The Teacher's Day in Bed

Our teacher's having a day in bed—
She's sent her pets to school instead!

There's . . .

A parrot to read the register,
A crocodile to sharpen the pencils,
A canary to teach singing,
An adder to teach maths,
An octopus to make the ink,
An elephant to hoover the floor,
An electric eel to make the computer work,
A giraffe to look for trouble at the back,
A tiger to keep order at the front,
A reed bunting (can't you guess?
to help with reeding, of course!),
A secretary bird to run the office
A piranha fish to give swimming lessons
(Glad I'm off swimming today!),
A zebra to help with crossing the road,
Oh, and a dragon to cook the sausages.

I bet that none of you ever knew
Just how many things a teacher can do!

David Orme

Louder!

OK, Andrew, nice and clearly—off you go.

Welcome everybody to our school concert . . .

Louder, please, Andrew. Mums and dad won't hear
you at the back, will they?

Welcome everybody to our school concert . . .

Louder, Andrew. You're not trying.
Pro–ject–your–voice.
Take a b i g b r e a t h and louder!

Welcome everybody to our school concert . . .

For goodness sake, Andrew. LOUDER! LOUDER!

Welcome every body to our school concert!

Now, Andrew, there's no need to be silly.

Roger Stevens

Captain to Captain

Winmoor School
Gamesborough
WEI URO

Dear Mark and the boys of Matcham School team,

As Captain of Winmoor football team may I thank you for the match. We all enjoyed the tussle and the goal we managed to snatch! Sorry about all the bruises, and your striker's broken left arm. Our defenders are normally so careful that their tackles don't do any harm.

I expect you were all really upset that the goalie's nose bled when it did, and that the full back, when making his challenge, scored a stunning home goal from his skid.

Although it was quite hard to beat you, we feel that our victory was fair. We hope that your boys are good losers—as for us, we'll just let down our hair!

Looking forward to the return match next season,

Best wishes,

Hannah,

on behalf of the team: Julie, Suzanne, Lucy, Emma, Molly, Sarah, Liz, Isabel, Katie, and Becky.

Daphne Kitching

The Wizard Said:

'You find a sheltered spot that faces south . . .'
  'And then?'
'You sniff and put two fingers in your mouth . . .'
  'And then?'
'You close your eyes and roll your eyeballs round . . .'
  'And then?'
'You lift your left foot slowly off the ground . . .'
  'And then?'
'You make your palm into a kind of cup . . .'
  'And then?'
'You *very quickly* raise your right foot up . . .'
  'And then?'
'You fall over.'

Richard Edwards

A Few Spells from
The Great Magician Mig-Mog

Abracadabra
wibble wobble woo,
I'm going to put you
into my stew!

Abracadabra
wibble wobble whee,
I'm going to gobble you up
for my tea!

Abracadabra
bibble bobble boodle,
you'd taste good
in a big pot noodle!

Abracadabra
bibble bobble bog . . .
                    whoops!
Oh dear, I've turned you
into a *FROG*!

Judith Nicholls

Cherry Croak

(*or* Raiding the Wizard's Kitchen)

Cor!
I wonder what this is for?
It's all red and fizzy,
just like cherry Coke
(except for the smoke . . .)

Hmmmm . . .
cool as ice.
Mmmmm . . .
smells nice.
Think, maybe
I'll try a sip.
Oooh! Bubbles bursting
on my lip—
Pop! Pop! Pop!

Heeeeey! Everything's taller.
Oh, no. It's me that's getting smaller.
Oooh! *Hop! Hop! Hop!*
Well, I'm blowed!
I've turned into a toad.
That was no Coke.
And this is no joke.
Croak, croak, croak . . .

Tony Mitton

Owl in a Huff

'Which witch
swooped down,'
said the owl,
'and scared the mouse
just as I
was about
to pounce?

If I find out
which witch it was
watch out!'

Patricia Leighton

The Trainee Witch

I'm a trainee witch,
my name is Joan
and today I tried
some spells on my own.

I tried to turn a cassette player
    into a cat
but it ended up
    as a cricket bat.

I tried to turn a tractor
    to a killer whale
but it ended up
    as a fingernail.

I tried to turn a lawnmower
    into a toad
but it ended up
    as a hole in the road.

I tried to turn a chimney
    to a fleet of ships
but it ended up
    as a bag of chips.

I tried to turn a television
    into a doll
but it ended up
    as a sausage roll.

I'm a trainee witch,
my name is Joan
but I'm not very good
at spells on my own.

Charles Thomson

A Bedtime Prayer

Protect me from vampires
Protect me from ghouls
Protect me from phantoms
And howling werewolves
Protect me from witches
Protect me from ghosts
Protect me from brother Sid
I fear him the most.

Richard Caley

Wigwise

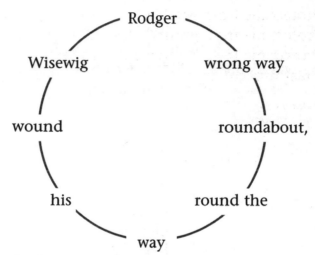

Rodger

Wisewig   wrong way

wound   roundabout,

his   round the

way

Gina Douthwaite

Oky Doky

OKY DOKY NIXY NOX
kept his auntie in a box.
Every Sunday, spruced and neat,
he took her walking for a treat.

How she chattered! How she went
on in endless argument!
He was glad when Monday came
and he could put her back again.

Jean Kenward

Cop This!

Uncle Ted
Is a plain clothes officer
In the London police force.

He is seven-foot tall
And his office
Is right at the top
Of New Scotland Yard.

So that must make him
Very
High Tec.

Trevor Harvey

Custard Pie

I'm Sidney Splatt the custard pie
I love the human race
And best of all I like to spread
Across its smiling face.

There isn't time to shout 'Look out!'
Or even 'What was that?'
Before I hit the target
Kersplosh! Kersplash! Kersplat!

Gareth Owen

www.ifail@r-i-p.com.uk

I'm not feeling well
I have an infection
I can't seem to download
Or make a connection.

It was an attachment
Which caused me to fail
Now I can't surf the web
Or send an e-mail.

I'm starting to sink
I've no Internet Link
And instead of completing
I just keep deleting.

Don't call me a dimwit
I've had a breakdown
Please, Close and Exit
Please! Shut me down!

I've lost all my functions
So please disconnect
And call the technicians
I'm totally wrecked.

The domain providers
Have threatened to fire us
For I'm a computer
Who caught a virus!

Brenda Williams

Ibble Obble

I once met an alien
Who said this to me:

Ibble Obble
Bibble Bobble
Bobble Bibble
Ip

Dibble Dobble
Zing bang bop
Bibble Bibble
Zip

Zibble zabble
I like scrabble
Dibble wibble
Dip

Ibble obble
Bibble bobble
Dibble nibble
Ip?

And I simple had to agree

Tony Bradman

Goodwill Message Received

Do not worry, earth people. Greetings.
We are Legolians from the planet Lego.
We are here to make contact and build a better
   place.
We have travelled many moons with our fellow
   brothers and sisters—
The Jigsaw Creatures.

Together we are looking to construct a bright and
   better future
And see the bigger, fuller picture.

Do not worry, earth people.
Do not be puzzled.
We have not come to harm you.
No . . . we come in pieces.

Paul Cookson

Watchwords

watch the words
watch words the
watchword is
watch words are   away
sly as boots
ifyoutakeyoureyesoffthemforaminute

        they're up and

          allover

       the

         place

Roger McGough

Night Mer

One night when I was fast apeels
all duggled snown and warm
I had a very dasty ream
about a stunder thorm
and fightning lashed
and saves at wea
like boiling werpents sithed
and foaming angs did frockle me
and shicked and slucked and eyethed.
They ulled me under, lungings full
of fevvered, fluffin fug
till suffing grably I apized
upon the redboom bug.

Gina Douthwaite

Reading in Reading

Kids with good books,
Kind homes and warm bedding
Will be so good at reading,
And live, maybe, near Reading.
If they knew new books
That they'd like to read,
Then ideas in their heads
Would quite rapidly breed.
Reading good books in Reading,
Understand what I've said,
Will make those who read them
Extremely well-read.

John Kitching

Sunnyside Up

When people
See people
Reading up
Side Down,
They think,
Maybe,
The reader
Can't read,
But
You should
Smile now,
Because you
Have found
A poem
That's out
To mislead.

Benjamin Zephaniah

The Eleph and the Ant

An unhappy tearful eleph
Stood in the mud and pined,
'The front of me's feeling all cut off,
It's lonely without a behind.'

It tried pinching the end from a curr***
The beginning from a tired ***elope
The middle from p***s and S***a
But they all whipped them back at a stroke.

Its tears dripped down on a notice
With 'WANTED' in letters of red,
All the jungle was there to toast them
When the eleph and ant were W   ED.

Gina Claye

Mo Use Mouse

What cheese does Mo use
In her sweet little house?
Does Mo use a cheese
She could feed to a mouse?

If Mo uses cheese
That is not very nice,
Would she feed it to mouses
Or feed it to mice?

If a goose had a brother,
A sister, a niece,
Would you then have three gooses,
Or maybe three geese?

And if it's three geese,
Could three moose be three meese?

From these weird wordy puzzles,
PLEASE! Quickly give me some peace!

John Kitching

Dinah Saw

Dinah saw eight dinosaurs
Eight dinosaurs saw Dinah
The dinosaurs that Dinah saw
Ate Dinah for their dinner.

Richard Caley

Was it a Cat I Saw?

Was it a cat I saw
Creeping behind the door?

Can you say this backwards?
  Wasitacatisaw?

Mike Jubb

Swimmerick

There was a young girl of Kilkee,
Who went for a swim in the ocean.
    When they said, 'Is it hot?'
    She replied, 'No, it isn't.
I could do with a nice cup of cocoa.'

Gerard Benson

Lim

There once was a bard of Hong Kong
Who thought limericks were too long.

Gerard Benson

Guy Fawkesed

One day after school,
my brother rushes up to me shouting,
'I know who Guy Fawkesed was.'
'Guy Fawkes,' I say.
'He was the man who tried to blowed up
THE HOUSES OF PARSLEY!'
'Er—Parliament, you mean.'
'Yes, with a—POW! BANG! BOOMED-DEE-BOOM-
    BOOM!'
'Really.'
'But then he was caughted!'
'You mean caught.'
'And then he was exe . . . exe . . . er . . . kill-ded by
    the kingy-thingy man.'
'Er . . . killed, and then what happened?'
'Well he was only kill-ded for a few days.'
'Oh yes.'
'Then the kingy tolded him he'd been a naughty,
    NAUGHTY man!'
'Y-es.'
'Then he tolded him not to do it ever-never again.'
'Well that was very kind of the king.'
'Yes, and then—he letted him go
and he lived happily ever after until the next day.'
'Aaah, I like nice endings!'

Ian Souter

I Don't Like My Brother in the Morning

Every morning on a Saturday and Sunday
I go to my paper round at 6.30 a.m.
and by 7.00 I am back home
and I go back to bed to get some sleep.
I make a little bit of noise
when I get into bed,
and just when I am dozing off,
my brother wakes up.
He knows I am awake
and he wants me to stay awake
so he goes outside for a pee—
I know that, because I can hear him
flush the toilet.
Then he bursts inside
and stands in front of the mirror
and says, 'SPIDER MAN!!!'

Keith Ballentine

Hi, I'm Ian

And so are my brothers—

This first brother writes down notes.
He's the Music-
Ian.
The next one wants your votes.
That's the Politic-
Ian.

The third turns dark to light.
The Electric-
Ian.
Then there's one who checks your sight.
Meet the Optic-
Ian.

My last brother cures the sick.
Here's the Physic-
Ian.
And me, I just do tricks.
I am the Magic-
Ian.

David Horner

A Letter to the Tooth Fairy

Here I am again
With another tooth for you.
It just came out,
It didn't hurt at all.

I've put a bit of salt on it
And wrapped it in silvery paper
Like Mum said.

Please take it away, and perhaps,
You could leave something
Like you did last time.

Oh yes!—
My little brother Ben
Hasn't any teeth at all
I'm sure he'd like some.

So!
I know you do take-aways.
I wonder,
If you do deliveries?

Thank you very much

Love

      Hannah.

David Whitehead

I'b Godda Gold

I'b godda gold,
whadebber I say
seebs do cum out
in uh nodd way.

I coff ud sneedz,
by dose id runny,
a gold like dis,
it id snot funny.

By ears are blogged,
by dose id raw,
by poor ead daches,
by throad id sore.

Dis rodden gold
bakes be feel blue,
but I'll be bedder
in uh day or do.

Jane Clarke

Plub Jab ad Barbalade

I've godda cold id by doze
And I cahn say plub jab,
Which id a shabe cus I lub plub jab.

Ad breakfast I cudd'nt say barbalade,
Which id a shabe cus I lub barbalade.

Sniff!

Ad the tug shob ad by school,
I cudd'nt say KidKad blease,
Which is a shabe cus I lub KidKads.

Sniff!

Ab subber time by Bub said 'wad do you wad'
I cudd'nt say plub jab,
Dor I cudd'nt say barbalade,
Ad I doh Bub wudden led be ave KidKads.

Sniff!

I cud say dry toast.
So I said dry toast blease Bub,
Which is sujjer shabe cus
I hade rodden ole dry toast.

David Whitehead

Nothing

I've got a present for you—here it is.
Yes, it's a big
load
of nothing.
I'd have wrapped it in shiny paper
but I couldn't find the time.

As you can see
it's flat on top
with smooth round sides
and when you put your hand into it
there's nothing there at all—
that's how full it is of nothing.

What do you mean—what use is it?
Nothing can do anything,
it's up to you:
you can eat it, you can drink it,
you can kick it, or stroke it,
you can put it on your head,
you can take it for a walk
or talk to it when you're alone,
and best of all
you can
think about it.

Here you are then—catch!
Now where's it gone?
Who's got nothing?

Dave Calder

My Hat!

Here's my hat.
It holds my head,
the thoughts I've had,
and the things I've read.

It keeps out the wind.
It keeps off the rain.
It hugs my hair
and warms my brain.

There's me below it,
the sky above it.
It's my lid.
And I love it.

Tony Mitton

Hair Growing

Hair grows a centimetre a month
Or a third of a millimetre a day.
That means
That while you've been reading these poems
Your hair
(And mine)
Will have grown
A billimetre,
A trillimetre,
A zillimetre
Or a squillimetre!
It depends how fast you read.

Sue Cowling

Foot Note

I'll tell you a secret
You mustn't repeat,
A secret about
My best friend's . . . feet.
I'm sorry to say
That my friend Ray's
Got feet that smell.
Oh, please don't tell—
He's a very good friend.
But his feet are . . .
      the end.

Tony Bradman

Index of titles/first lines

(First lines in italic)

ACKNOWLEDGEMENTS

We are grateful for permission to reproduce the following poems:

John Agard: 'Mother Alligator's Advice to Her Children' from *I Din Do Nuttin* (Bodley Head, 1983), reprinted by permission of The Random House Group Ltd. **Gerard Benson:** 'Yum!' from *Evidence of Elephants* (Viking, 1995) and 'Lim', copyright © Gerard Benson 1990. from E O Parrott (ed): *How to be Well-Versed in Poetry* (Viking, 1990), both reprinted by permission of the author. **Tracey Blance:** 'I Don't Know What to Write', copyright © Tracey Blance 2000, first published in Paul Cookson (ed): *The Works* (Macmillan Children's Books, 2000), reprinted by permission of the author. **Margaret Blount:** 'Riddle', copyright © Margaret Blount 1993, first published in Brian Moses (ed): *My First Has Gone Bonkers* (Blackie, 1993), reprinted by permission of the author. **Tony Bradman:** 'Ibble Obble' and 'Foot Note' from *Smile Please* (Viking Kestrel, 1987), copyright © Tony Bradman 1987, reprinted by permission of Penguin Books Ltd. **Richard Caley:** 'A Bedtime Prayer', copyright © Richard Caley 2000, first published in Paul Cookson (ed): *The Works* (Macmillan Children's Books, 2000), reprinted by permission of the author. **Charles Causley:** 'Good Morning, Mr Croco-Doco-Dile' from *Collected Poems for Children* (Macmilan), reprinted by permission of David Higham Associates. **Peter Dixon:** 'Where Do All the Teachers Go?' from *Grow Your Own Poems* (Peche Luna), copyright © Peter Dixon 1988, reprinted by permission of the author. **Gina Douthwaite:** 'Night Mer', copyright © Gina Douthwaite 1998, first published in Paul Cookson (ed): *Unzip Your Lips* (Macmillan Children's Books, 1998), reprinted by permission of the author. **Richard Edwards:** 'The Wizard Said' from *The Word Party* (Lutterworth, 1987), reprinted by permission of the author. **Max Fatchen:** 'Be Nice to Rhubarb' from *Songs for My Dog and Other People* (Kestrel, 1980), copyright © Max Fatchen 1980, reprinted by permission of John Johnson (Authors' Agent) Ltd. **David Horner:** 'Hi, I'm Ian', copyright © David Horner 2001, from *Happy to Be Here* (Apple Pie Publications, 2001), reprinted by permission of the author. **Roger McGough:** 'Watchwords' from *Watchwords* (Jonathan Cape, 1969), copyright © Roger McGough 1969, reprinted by permission of PFD on behalf of Roger McGough. **Tony Mitton:** 'Cherry Croak' and 'My Hat!' from *Plum* (Scholastic Children's Books, 1998), reprinted by permission of David Higham Associates. **David Orme:** 'The Teacher's Day in Bed', copyright © David Orme 2000, first published in Paul Cookson (ed): *The Works* (Macmillan Children's Books, 2000), reprinted by permission of the author. **Roger Stevens:** 'Louder!', copyright © Roger Stevens 1996, first published in Pie Corbett (ed): *Custard Pie* (Macmillan Children's Books, 1996), reprinted by permission of the author. **Charles Thomson:** 'The Trainee Witch' from *Never Say Boo to a Ghost* (OUP, 1990), copyright © Charles Thomson 1990, reprinted by permission of the author. **Celia Warren:** 'Elephantasy', copyright © Celia Warren 1994, from Judith Nicholls (ed): *A Trunkful of Elephants* (Methuen, 1994), and 'The Yeti', copyright © Celia Warren 1999, from *Never Sit on a Squid* (Ginn, 1999), both reprinted by permission of the author. **Benjamin Zephaniah:** 'Multi-Culture' and 'Sunnyside Up' from *Talking Turkeys* (Viking Kestrel, 1994), copyright © Benjamin Zephaniah 1994, reprinted by permission of Penguin Books Ltd.

All other poems are published for the first time in this collection by permission of their authors.

Gerard Benson: 'Swimmerick', copyright © Gerard Benson 2001 **Liz Brownlee:** 'Hippobotamus', copyright © Liz Brownlee 2001 **Dave Calder:** 'Nothing', copyright © Dave Calder 2001 **Richard Caley:** 'My Newt', 'Why Does Rhubarb Crumble?', and 'Dinah Saw', copyright © Richard Caley 2001 **Alison Chisholm:** 'Octocure', copyright © Alison Chisholm 2001 **Jane Clarke:** 'I'b Godda Gold', copyright © Jane Clarke 2001 **Gina Claye:** 'The Eleph and the Ant', copyright © Gina Claye 2001 **Paul Cookson:** 'Goodwill Message Received', copyright © Paul Cookson 2001 **Sue Cowling:** 'The Laughter Forecast' and 'Hair Growing', copyright © Sue Cowling 2001 **Gina Douthwaite:** 'Wigwise' , copyright © Gina Douthwaite 2001 **Trevor Harvey:** 'Cop This', copyright © Trevor Harvey 2001 **Maureen Haselhurst:** 'Just a Tad', copyright © Maureen Haselhurst 2001 **Mike Jubb:** 'Was It a Cat I Saw?', copyright © Mike Jubb 2001 **Jean Kenward:** 'Oky Doky', copyright © Jean Kenward 2001 **Daphne Kitching:** 'Captain to Captain', copyright © Daphne Kitching 2001 **John Kitching:** 'Reading in Reading' and 'Mo Use Mouse', copyright © John Kitching 2001 **Patricia Leighton:** 'Owl in a Huff', copyright © Patricia Leighton 2001 **Colin Macfarlane:** 'The Dinosaur', copyright © Colin Macfarlane 2001 **Ray Mather:** 'Lolly Licking', copyright © Ray Mather 2000 **Trevor Millum:** 'Brian and the Lion', copyright © Trevor Millum 2001 **Judith Nicholls:** 'A Few Spells from the Great Magician Mig-Mog', copyright © Judith Nicholls 2001 **Gareth Owen:** 'Custard Pie', copyright © Gareth Owen 2001 **Matt Simpson:** 'My Painting', copyright © Matt Simpson 2001 **Ian Souter:** 'Guy Fawkesed', copyright © Ian Souter 2001 **Marion Swinger:** 'Well Spotted', copyright © Marion Swinger 2001 **Clive Webster:** 'A Froggy was Sitting Crying', copyright © Clive Webster 2001 **David Whitehead:** 'Letter to the Tooth Fairy' and 'Plub Jab ad Barbelade', copyright © David Whitehead 2001 **Brenda Williams:** 'www.ifail@r-i-p.com.uk', copyright © Brenda Williams 2001

Despite every effort to try to trace and contact copyright holders before publication this has not been possible in every case. If notified the publisher will be pleased to rectify any errors or omissions at the earliest opportunity.